Of the Earth, Stars, and Coffee

Daniel Werbowsky

BookLeaf Publishing
India | USA | UK

Presentation by *BookLeaf Publishing*

Web: www.bookleafpub.com

E-mail: info@bookleafpub.com

ISBN: 9789357446921

First edition 2022

DEDICATION

For you.

With all that I am, I thank you.

I love you.

Autumn's Palette

And so I sit and sip
my coffee, still hot.
Looking over the town,
my mind drifts...
as does the breeze,
and fall takes hold.

The sunrise so lovely,
looks like October.
Purple-pink into blue.
Golden rays...
through fractured clouds,
warm the city.

Some leaves sit on the ground...
though most are still green.
That will change soon enough,
and yellows...
and browns will fill
Autumn's palette.

rain refresh

Blissful and lost
in the spring rain,
the torrent
of light, wet and twisted
wiped from your brow.
Replaced
and wiped away once more.

A galaxy of raindrops
placing themselves with intent.
like fingers on a fretboard,
they drip and drag.
That delightful symphonic impression
You're blissfully lost
in the sweet spring rain.

the lost

Each star
dotting the purple/black
Is a setting Sun
watched
by romantics
and the lost

untitled

once the rain gets here
the sky will grow dark
and the pink horizon
will be yours alone.

the deep breath of night
will allow the stars
to sparkle and dance
'til morning's exhale

My Day of Pretty Things

Finding myself inside a grin
with no reason or cause
or purpose to stop.
Such delight, I've found
in a day of pretty things.

A Sweet Longing

Dreaming sweet...
she's a Siren,
singing a song
only he can hear__
eyes on the horizon
feels an ocean apart.
He stands by the shore.

A Morning Moment

A warm sky kissed pink
by an embarrassed sunrise
beguiles the cool damp grass
into which she wiggles her toes.

A cradled coffee mug
ads to the dancing fog
that blankets the lake
across which she stares.

Hearing the morning's song
and bringing the mug to her lips
the morning issues a calm
with which she begins her day.

Dreams

Imagine...
falling asleep under a starry sky...
only to float into a dream so sweet
to make your pink lips curl.

Fingertips to your neck...
you smile yourself awake.
catch your breath
as your vision clears
there they are
still feeling as though twirling
through a dream...
your stars,
they dance.

Foothold

Regardless
how still the surface
how strong your footing
the water is still flowing
beneath the ice.

She

waking with a sunrise
she floats the steam with her breath
her lips to ceramic rim
she grins

eyes closed with sweet inhale
her playful grin peeks out
a graceful sight so lovely
she's warm

it's a funny thing
little scenes like this
so often it happens
yet so easily missed

set against a sunset
the scenery moves with her
pinks, yellows, both sky and skin
she dreams

and when the starry light
reaches the curve of her neck
elegance sets me back
she's light

While it Rains

it's raining
it's raining and I'm thinking of you
with each raindrop rattling my window
a memory dances it's way
to the front of my mind

they race down the windowpane
and my heart keeps pace
lost in the thirst for that water
I write to you in hope
you think of me..
when it rains

The Cup I Poured

I waited too long
my coffee has run cold
no steam left to drift
still, the smell prompts me to sip.
Though I could make another,
this is the cup I poured.
So, sip it I will.
I just waited too long.

Springtime Night

Lay yourself down
amongst the tall grass
it's just you
and a billion points of light

Give yourself time
to notice the Moon
She's up there
but no nearer the stars

Perspective granted
the story goes
the night's breeze floats in
tickles your nose...

The Earthly Love

I'm reminded of the sky
Sun spinning
yet still
stars fixed
yet rotate and tilt.

the earthly love
unraveled
from the cosmic tangle.

Garden

You are a garden.
Be a garden,
awash
with love...
and subtle beauty.
Let passersby be.
Take root,
as suits you true.
Reach out,
to only your Sun,
to only your rain.
Absorb the flood
and bloom...
just bloom.

Yellow

What's a boy to do?
I see her
gathering yellow flowers
They bloomed the Sun.
It Zig-Zag'd that day.

Oh, Beautiful Day

Oh, sweet!
Oh, beautiful day!
watch the water
with the sand between your toes.

Listen to the tales she tells
between the waves
that silence calls out
to you.

What she tells you
only you know.
it's a song sung
to you alone.

Ocean child...
Saltwater lips...
Oh, sweet!
Oh, beautiful day!

Goodnights

Goodnights gone elsewhere
I cannot take credit
for a pretty sky
she weeps and shines
all on her own.

Cherry Tree

The cherries are in.
sour...
though, I'll eat all I can.
get them before the birds.
greedy, they'll get their share.
the tree is taller,
than I can reach.
sour...
those cherries I love.

2020

I find myself
watching in wonder
as an invisible wind
shifts the branches.

They will be still
once more.
once the breeze
takes it's sleep.

note/hope

With each wave
comes a note
and a hope
and a timeless melody.